The Campus History Series

FRESNO PACIFIC UNIVERSITY
THE FIRST 75 YEARS

KEVIN ENNS-REMPEL AND HANNAH KEENEY

Fresno Pacific University

75 YEARS

1944-2019

During the 2019–2020 academic year, Fresno Pacific University celebrates its 75th anniversary. In three quarters of a century, it has grown from a tiny Bible institute almost exclusively for students in the Mennonite Brethren Church to a leading institution of higher education in California's Central Valley. (Courtesy of Fresno Pacific University, Hiebert Library archives.)

ON THE COVER: Students study in Hiebert Library sometime in the early 1960s. Today, this part of the library is filled with shelves for the reference and periodical sections. (Courtesy of Fresno Pacific University, Hiebert Library archives.)

ON THE BACK COVER: Students are gathered near the Rebekah Fountain north of the Science Building (now known as Marpeck Center) around 1968. (Courtesy of Fresno Pacific University, Hiebert Library archives.)

The Campus History Series

Fresno Pacific University
The First 75 Years

Kevin Enns-Rempel and Hannah Keeney

Copyright © 2020 by Kevin Enns-Rempel and Hannah Keeney
ISBN 978-1-4671-0459-3

Published by Arcadia Publishing
Charleston, South Carolina

Library of Congress Control Number: 2019947444

For all general information, please contact Arcadia Publishing:
Telephone 843-853-2070
Fax 843-853-0044
E-mail sales@arcadiapublishing.com
For customer service and orders:
Toll-Free 1-888-313-2665

Visit us on the Internet at www.arcadiapublishing.com

Contents

Acknowledgments	6
Introduction	7
1. Pacific Bible Institute: 1944–1960	9
2. Pacific College: 1960–1976	35
3. Fresno Pacific College: 1976–1997	69
4. Fresno Pacific University: 1997–present	99

Acknowledgments

Thank you to Eugene Enns and the other members of the Fresno Pacific University 75th Anniversary Executive Committee for approving this project. We also are grateful to the staff of Hiebert Library for indulging us as we worked on this book rather than other library projects. Wayne Steffen provided invaluable assistance in reading the manuscript for content, tone, and grammar.

All photographs are from the university archives in Hiebert Library.

INTRODUCTION

In its 75-year history, Fresno Pacific University has encompassed a remarkable, perhaps even bewildering, set of identities and structures. Its main campus has been at three different locations: in Fresno's Tower District, in downtown Fresno, and now in southeast Fresno. It has offered programs at regional campuses at more than a dozen locations since the mid-1990s in four Central Valley cities: north Fresno, Visalia, Bakersfield, and Merced. It has had four different names: Pacific Bible Institute, Pacific College, Fresno Pacific College, and Fresno Pacific University. It began as an unaccredited Bible institute, evolved from that into a junior college, then a four-year liberal arts college, and today a university offering a wide variety of undergraduate, continuing education, and graduate programs. Its founding vision was to train lay leaders for work in Mennonite Brethren churches, with little expectation that students from other Christian traditions would someday be a significant part of the student body. Over time, that vision would expand beyond anything the founders could imagine. Today, only a very small percentage of the students are members of the Mennonite Brethren Church, and students from racial minority groups make up the majority of the enrollment.

The theological orientation of the university has also changed noticeably since 1944. In its earliest form, the Bible institute was very much shaped by American fundamentalism, though it also sought to inculcate students with traditional Mennonite practices such as "nonconformity" and "nonresistance." With the shift away from a Bible institute model in the early 1960s, Pacific College also embraced a new identity as an Anabaptist-Mennonite institution. While the Mennonite Brethren identity had been part of the institution's ethos from the very first, only in the 1960s did the college seek to place that specific denominational identity into the larger theological context of Anabaptism. The document known as the "Pacific College Idea" (today the "Fresno Pacific University Idea" but hereafter simply called the "Idea"), written in 1966, clearly set the college within that theological framework. While the Anabaptist identity remains one of the most important identifying features of Fresno Pacific University today, it has also come to embrace a much greater degree of theological diversity in recent years. Today, it is common for the university to speak of itself as simultaneously being evangelical, Anabaptist, and ecumenical. While these three terms are seldom used to describe a single institution, part of the dynamic identity that Fresno Pacific has fostered comes from its attempt to weave these strands together into a single cord.

The founders of Pacific Bible Institute sought to maintain a sense of denominational loyalty in their students and protect them from what they understood to be the corrosive effects of the larger society. They required that all students accept the faith statements of the institute, whether or not they were members of the Mennonite Brethren Church. By the 1960s, this kind of boundary maintenance had largely been replaced by a different educational philosophy, one that sought to equip students to bring a Christian faith perspective to their interactions with the larger cultural, scientific, and intellectual world. Since the 1960s, the university has encouraged a voluntary acceptance of its faith commitments but has stipulated no requirements that students must personally hold those beliefs. Faculty and staff, however, must demonstrate an active Christian belief.

The board structure that governs the university has also changed significantly during these first 75 years. Pacific Bible Institute was founded by the Pacific District Conference of Mennonite Brethren Churches (which included all Mennonite Brethren congregations in California, Oregon, and Washington), and that conference elected the institute's board for the first 10 years. In 1954, the Mennonite Brethren Church in the United States reorganized its educational structures and created a unified Board of Education to oversee both Pacific Bible Institute and its sister institution Tabor College in Hillsboro, Kansas (and also the Mennonite Brethren Biblical Seminary when it was established in 1955). This structure remained in place for 25 years, until the US Conference of Mennonite Brethren Churches voted to regionalize its schools in 1979. Fresno Pacific thus returned to an affiliation with the Pacific District, the conference that had founded it in 1944.

So many changing identities and structures might lead to the conclusion that Fresno Pacific University has had little clear focus or continuity in its first 75 years, but that would be incorrect. It has remained unapologetically a Christian institution of higher education. In the words of the "Idea," it seeks to be "centered upon Christ and His church," and is "committed to the ideals of God's Kingdom." The university

> Affirms the authority of the Bible over all matters of faith and life; the church as a community of redeemed people; a life of discipleship leading to holiness, witness, and service; the call to serve Jesus by ministering to human need and alleviating suffering; the practice of reconciliation and love in settings of violence, oppression, and injustice; and the development of spiritual maturity through disciplines such as prayer, study, and meditation.

These values and beliefs have characterized the institution since its very beginning and will continue to shape its identity for the future.

This 75th-anniversary history uses photographic images taken from the university's archival collection to tell the story of Fresno Pacific University since 1944. As with any photographic history, the narrative has been inevitably shaped by the things that people chose to record in photographs and the fact that some aspects of campus life have been more thoroughly documented than others. The authors have done their best to tell the university's story in the most balanced way possible within the limits of its medium.

The book has been divided into chapters defined by the four names of the institution since 1944. While the new names themselves did not bring about the institutional changes described here, they do closely correspond to those changes. The decision to adopt a new name in each case has at least implicitly (and sometimes explicitly) been a recognition of a new institutional identity. The photographs on the pages that follow trace both changes and the enduring vision that has characterized Fresno Pacific University from its beginnings to the present day.

One

PACIFIC BIBLE INSTITUTE
1944–1960

The institution known today as Fresno Pacific University was born in 1944 as Pacific Bible Institute. It was created by the Pacific District Conference of Mennonite Brethren Churches, a denomination that included only about 10,400 members in the entire United States, less than 4,000 of whom lived on the West Coast. This small denomination had already founded Tabor College in Hillsboro, Kansas, in 1908. How anyone thought that such a small denomination could support two colleges is hard to imagine. And yet that tiny group of Mennonite Brethren churches on the West Coast decided to take on the challenge of creating its own school. In 1935, the Pacific District created a School and Education Committee, and in 1941 accepted the committee's recommendation to establish a Bible institute. The conference chose the name Pacific Bible Institute for its new school in 1943. In February 1944, a large residence on Van Ness Avenue was purchased as the first campus, and classes met for the first time in the fall of 1944.

By 1946, the Bible institute had already outgrown its original facilities and moved into a larger building in downtown Fresno. Enrollment continued to rise during the first several years, but by the early 1950s, had reached a plateau and soon began to decline. Apparently, the desire for a narrowly defined Bible institute curriculum was not as strong among Mennonite Brethren young people as the school's founders had imagined.

While the future of the Bible institute remained very much in doubt, its leaders continued to plan for a better future. They proposed a new liberal arts curriculum that offered a path beyond the original Bible institute model. The decision in 1955 to purchase land in southeast Fresno for a new campus was further evidence that many held hope for a brighter future.

On September 18, 1944, students, faculty, board members, parents, and other supporters of Pacific Bible Institute gathered on the steps of 1095 N. Van Ness Avenue, in what today is known as Fresno's Tower District. They came together to celebrate the institute's opening day of classes with songs, prayer, and inspiring messages. Twenty-eight students were enrolled in the first study body, and four full-time faculty members taught almost all classes in the curriculum. Virtually the entire student body consisted of young people from nearby Mennonite Brethren churches, with over half coming from the nearby churches in Reedley and Dinuba. From the very beginning, there were a few students from other Protestant denominations, but the mandate clearly was to train Mennonite Brethren students for work in their local churches. Three of the four faculty members were Mennonite Brethren ministers, as befit a curriculum focused almost entirely on theology, biblical studies, and Christian ministry subjects.

The building in which Pacific Bible Institute (PBI) made its first home was originally the residence of James Porteous, whose chief claim to fame was as the inventor of an earth-moving implement known as the "Fresno Scraper." As used by PBI, the building included an entrance hall, three classrooms, library, kitchen, service porch, a bathroom on the main floor, and seven rooms for girls' dormitories with two bathrooms upstairs.

Four students play basketball in the back yard of the Van Ness Avenue campus sometime around 1944–1945. Though originally designed as a large single-family home, the building had been remodeled as a boarding house after the original owners moved away. There were 24 people living in the home when PBI purchased it in 1944. The plumbing visible on the outside walls is probably evidence of remodeling done to accommodate additional residents.

The original Pacific Bible Institute faculty members stand on the steps of the Van Ness campus during the first academic year, 1944–1945. From left to right are Jacob J. Toews, Erwin E. Hofer, administrator Sam W. Goossen, and Sam Wiens. Of these four, only Goossen was still part of the faculty by the following academic year, evidence of the difficulty that PBI had in hiring and retaining faculty members during its early years.

Five of the seven original board members gathered for this photograph on the Van Ness campus steps sometime during 1944–1945. From left to right are treasurer Jacob D. Hofer, secretary Henry D. Wiebe, vice-chairman John H. Richert, David Letkeman, and chairman August A. Schroeter. Not pictured are board members Peter N. Hiebert and Henry Hooge.

The faculty (center of back row) and students pose on the steps of the Van Ness Avenue campus during the second semester of the first academic year. The number of female students (23) compared to male students (8) is almost certainly a result of World War II, which had forced many men into military service or (as was often the case for Mennonites) Civilian Public Service. While the students in this photograph may look like typical Americans of the time, they were very much part of an ethnoreligious immigrant group still working through its own acculturation process to mainstream American society. The Mennonite Brethren had come to the United States from Ukraine as German-speaking immigrants in the 1870s and had spent much of the next 70 years in rural enclaves that allowed them to control the acculturation process. Mennonite Brethren churches were still worshipping in German until the early 1940s. The Bible institute, however, conducted its curriculum in English and was one of the ways in which Mennonite Brethren young people adapted to the larger world.

The building on Van Ness quickly became too small for the Pacific Bible Institute program. And so, in 1946, PBI purchased a former YWCA recreation center at the corner of Tuolumne and L Streets in downtown Fresno for a new campus location. The building was originally designed by Julia Morgan, who is best known as the architect of Hearst Castle on the Central California coast. This building housed all school functions except for men's dormitories from 1946 until 1959. In its basement was a swimming pool, a feature that likely would not have been included if the school had designed the building itself. The most prominent feature added to the exterior of the building by PBI was a neon "Jesus Saves" sign on one corner. Apparently, this sign caused some passers-by to assume that the building was a rescue mission, with some occasionally coming inside to seek various forms of assistance. The sign was, perhaps fittingly, later purchased by the Merced Rescue Mission for around $100.

These images show the Tuolumne Street building as it looked from the street and inside its central courtyard. The building had many beautiful features, including the open-air courtyard flanked by French doors and arches, an auditorium with seating for 500, elaborately cross-beamed ceilings, fireplaces with colored brick and tile detailing, and what the *Fresno Bee* once referred to as "quaint little Juliet balconies" in front of the second-floor windows. While the building still exists today, none of these features are still evident. After Pacific College sold it in the early 1960s, the subsequent owner remodeled it beyond recognition as a Julia Morgan design.

This photograph shows a group of students meeting in Room 11 for the Mennonite Brethren Church history class during the 1950–1951 school year. The even split between male and female students shown here is indicative of how the student body had changed after the end of the war. By 1948, men outnumbered women, a situation that would not change again until 1978.

Four students and a recording engineer record a song for the *Pacific Bible Institute Hour* radio broadcast during the 1950–1951 year. The institute's presence on radio began in 1947, when the school chorus was invited to sing on a few local stations. Later, PBI was given the opportunity to produce a regular radio broadcast through KRDU in Dinuba. The radio broadcasts continued throughout much of the PBI era.

Students were encouraged to support global mission work through participation in Mission Prayer Bands, which met for weekly prayer meetings and organized one mission rally during each school year. Here, the Latin American Prayer Band for 1958–1959 presents a program for its rally. While the practice of white students emulating other cultures is almost universally considered inappropriate today, it was a common aspect of mission rhetoric at this time.

Christian service in the local community was a major part of the student experience at Pacific Bible Institute. Many students performed their required service in one of the His Jewels Bible Clubs, which offered Christian education to children in local communities. Here, Bible club teacher Elsie Friesen is seen in 1947 with students of the South Tulip Street class in south Fresno.

In 1947, George W. Peters was appointed the first actual president of Pacific Bible Institute. During its first three years, PBI had been led by acting administrators Sam W. Goossen and George B. Huebert, and so Peters's appointment represented a significant step forward in administrative stability. Shortly before his appointment at PBI, Peters had earned his PhD from the Kennedy School of Missions in Hartford, Connecticut, and was the first member of PBI's faculty to hold that degree. Under Peters's leadership, the institute received accreditation from the Accrediting Association of Bible Institutes and Colleges. Peters resigned as president in 1952, though he remained on the institute (and later seminary) faculty until 1958, even serving as dean for some time. He would later go on to a career as a well-known missiologist with a faculty position at Dallas Theological Seminary.

One of the most significant spaces on the Tuolumne Street campus was the auditorium, located on the ground floor. It was used for many purposes, including the student banquet shown here. For this event, the dining area appears to be surrounded by a low wall meant to signify that they were sailing in a large boat. Across the boat's bow is the figure of Jesus, leading them in a small sailboat. Events conducted in the auditorium included regular chapel services, music performances, radio broadcast performances, social events, physical education classes, and commencement ceremonies. Local Mennonite Brethren churches were also invited to use the space for evangelistic services or choir festivals.

The entire student body, faculty, and staff gathered during the 1951–1952 school year for this photograph on the front steps of the Fresno Memorial Auditorium in downtown Fresno, about four blocks away from the Tuolumne Street campus. Enrollment during this year was 136, slightly lower than the PBI-era peak of 161 in 1949–1950. The enrollment would

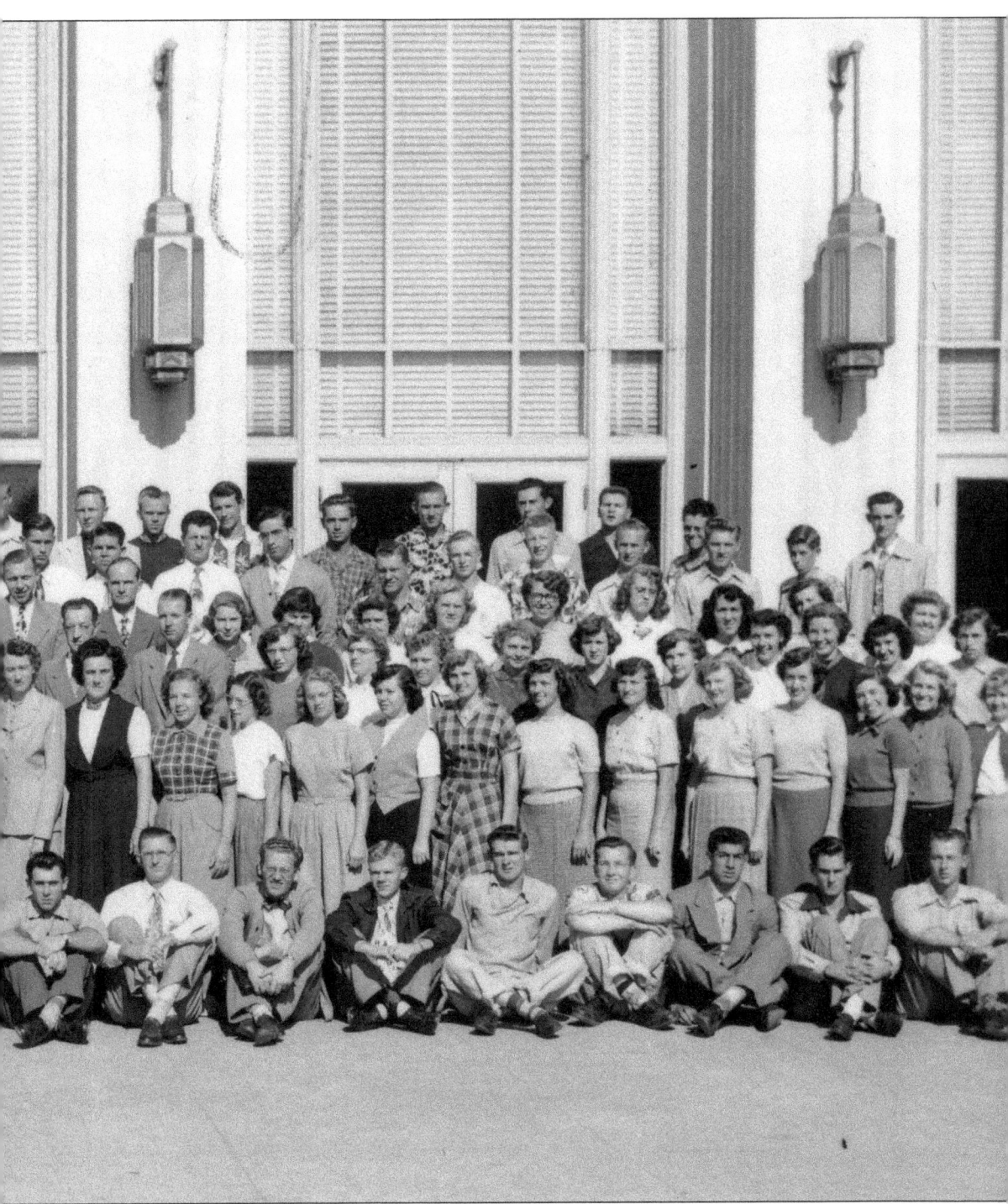
continue to decline for the rest of the 1950s, a reality that led the board to move away from the Bible institute program and instead develop a liberal arts college program. It would take a decade, however, until enrollment again exceeded the number seen here.

From its very beginning, music was a prominent part of Pacific Bible Institute's curriculum and ministry. While musical expression took many forms, the choir was perhaps the most important. Here, music director Dietrich Friesen (right) stands with the 1953–1954 choir. With 21 members, the choir represented almost 20 percent of the total student body for that year.

Athletics was a very insignificant part of student life during the Pacific Bible Institute years. The school offered a small number of physical education classes (including badminton in the auditorium and swimming classes in the basement pool). The only competitive sports option was basketball. The team, apparently known as the "Messengers," competed mainly in church leagues during these years. Games were played in local community gymnasiums.

The library for the Tuolumne Street campus was located in two rooms on the second floor—one for a reading room and circulation desk (seen here) and another for book stacks. By 1958–1959, when this photograph was taken, the library had a collection of approximately 11,000 volumes. The librarian at the time was Mathilda Fast. She worked with just a few student assistants, such as the one seen here.

The main Tuolumne Street building had dormitories for single women, but nothing for men or married couples. At first, male students lived in various downtown houses leased by the institute. In 1949, PBI completed apartments on Hedges Avenue, about two and a half miles from the campus. The new facilities included 10 apartments for married couples and rooms for 60 single men. Here, Josie Janzen stands on the porch of an apartment.

Following the resignation of Pres. G.W. Peters in 1952, Pacific Bible Institute was led by a temporary Executive Committee of the School, chaired by Dean Rueben M. Baerg. In the spring of 1953, Baerg was appointed acting president. He served in that role until 1954 and would later return as a member of the seminary faculty in the late 1950s and early 1960s.

Olive Warkentin, here working in the office at the Tuolumne Street campus, became a part of the PBI staff in 1951. She served as office secretary and later dean of women. She briefly left the college in 1964 when she married Cornelius Hiebert, but returned as administrative assistant to the president after her husband's death in 1965. She retired from the school in 1983.

In 1955, the Board of Education purchased land near the corner of Chestnut and Butler Avenues for a new campus. The aerial view above looking north shows the property and surrounding area at the time of purchase. The area with densely planted tall trees is where the Seminary House, North Hall, Wiebe Education Center, and Bartsch Hall stand today. The empty fields to the east and south of that area would remain undeveloped until 1958, when construction finally began on the new campus. Signs announcing the future campus development were posted on various parts of the property, including the one below on Butler Avenue.

Most of the land purchased in 1955 was being used for agricultural purposes, but near the northwest corner stood one very imposing residence. This house had been built in 1916–1917 for Wylie M. Giffen, who at one time was purported to be the largest raisin grape farmer in the world. Giffen's fortunes took a turn for the worse in the 1920s, and he lost the house. It passed through a few other hands over the next decades before the Board of Education purchased the land on which it stood. Even though construction on the new campus was still a few years away, the board decided that the Giffen Home could be used almost immediately for the newly established Mennonite Brethren Biblical Seminary. The seminary moved from the Tuolumne Street campus into the house in the fall of 1956. It was large enough for all classrooms, a small library, offices, and even residential space for the president and his family.

After a brief period of interim leadership, Bernhard J. Braun was appointed president of both Pacific Bible Institute and the new seminary. An influential leader in the North American Mennonite Brethren Church, Braun was a logical choice as president of the denomination's first seminary. He had been the moderator of the North American Mennonite Brethren Conference from 1948 to 1954 and also served as the chairman of the Board of Reference and Counsel, which oversaw all questions of theology and church practices in the conference. Braun furthermore had been a pastor of the nearby Dinuba Mennonite Brethren Church for about a decade before becoming president, a congregation that was one of the school's most significant supporters in the early years.

The early seminary faculty is seen here around 1960 for a meeting in one of the classrooms. From left to right are Pres. B.J. Braun, William Bass, G.W. Peters, D. Edmond Hiebert, Henry Harder, Arthur G. Willems, and P.R. Lange. Hiebert was completely deaf, and it appears that Henry Harder is writing notes for him so that he can follow the proceedings.

During its first year, the seminary used the existing PBI library at the Tuolumne campus. That no longer was practical after moving to the Giffen Home. About 1,200 volumes were transferred from the main library to the seminary, primarily Bible commentaries, works in theology, Bible dictionaries, and biblical encyclopedias. The library (seen here) was placed in the former dining room, immediately behind the grand entrance lobby.

The 55 acres purchased in 1955 for the new campus site included almost all property between Butler Avenue on the north, Chestnut Avenue on the west, Hamilton Avenue on the south, and either Winery or Willow Avenues on the east. Realizing that it had no money with which to build facilities on the new campus and assuming that it would never need so much land anyway, the board decided to devote 20 acres to the campus, set aside three acres for a Mennonite Brethren Church, and subdivide the rest for residential development. Income from the sale of these lots would provide funds for campus development. This view of Townsend Avenue as seen from the seminary building shows construction underway on the Butler Avenue Mennonite Brethren Church (left) and several of the Campus Homesites houses. While the assumption that income was needed for construction was accurate, the board greatly underestimated how much land the school eventually would need. In the years since selling the residential lots, Fresno Pacific University has purchased back almost all of them west of Winery Avenue.

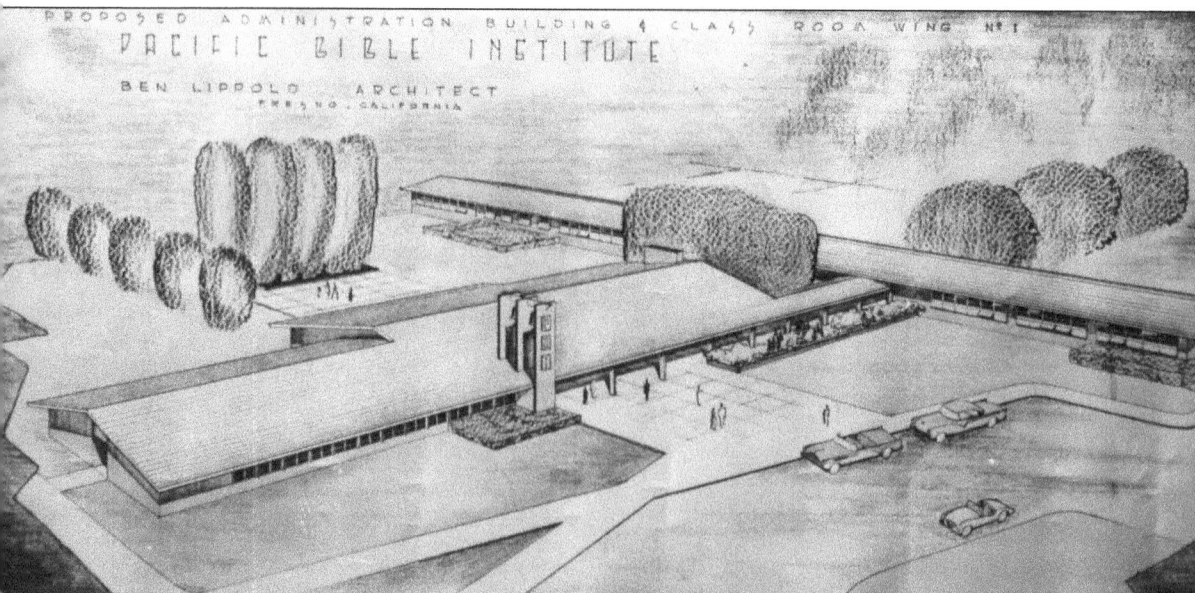

The board hired several local architects to draw site plan proposals for the new campus. Out of that process, Benjamin Franklin Lippold was hired to be the campus architect. Lippold had recently been chosen to design a new campus for Reedley College, and this fact undoubtedly had attracted the attention of the many Pacific Bible Institute supporters who lived in that area. He also had developed a reputation in the Central Valley for his public school designs, and his earliest drawings for the institute campus bore a strong resemblance to elementary school facilities. Among the many drawings that Lippold prepared was this sketch for a classroom/administration building to be located near a Chestnut Avenue campus entrance. This drawing appears on the cover of the 1956–1957 student yearbook, a vision of what they hoped would soon become reality. While the classroom wing would be built roughly in the form shown here, the administrative wing was never built.

The Board of Education, more concerned with funding construction on the campus of Tabor College in Kansas, offered Pacific Bible Institute no funds with which to begin development of the new Chestnut Avenue campus. This news, reported in April 1958, led to a discouraged mood among the Bible institute's supporters. The board did, however, give President Braun authorization to directly solicit loans and donations for that purpose. Braun was successful in this regard, and construction on a new classroom building (today known as Sattler Hall) began in the fall of 1958. Much of the work was performed by local volunteers under the leadership of Reedley contractor Sam Knaak. The building was completed in about seven months and dedicated on May 24, 1959.

The new classroom building had a stark appearance set all alone in the middle of plowed fields with only a tiny bit of lawn and a few saplings to break the emptiness. The seminary building, nestled in its heavily wooded corner, was the only other sign of a campus to be seen. Since one small building was inadequate for the needs of the school, students and

faculty shuttled back and forth between Tuolumne Street and Chestnut Avenue between 1959 and 1961. Classes were taught in the new Chestnut Avenue building, while the library, cafeteria, and dormitories remained at Tuolumne Street.

The new classroom building actually served multiple purposes. It had seven classrooms (one of which is shown here), a radio recording room, faculty and administrative offices, music practice rooms, restrooms, and a janitorial room. The interior finish was mahogany paneling, with acoustical tile ceilings and vinyl floors. Each room had an electric clock synchronized with the other clocks in the building, which in 1959 must have seemed quite remarkable.

One of the most novel spaces in the new building was a science classroom. Its inclusion was a sign that Pacific Bible Institute was moving forward with a new liberal arts curriculum that it hoped would reverse declining enrollments. Here, recently hired science professor Donald Braun provides instruction for students Louise Neufeld and Dwight Elrich shortly after completion of the new facilities.

Two

PACIFIC COLLEGE
1960–1976

The weakness of the Bible institute model had been evident for several years when the Board of Education asked Arthur Wiebe, a former administrator at Immanuel Academy in Reedley and a PhD candidate in mathematics at Stanford University, to consult with them about the school's future. Wiebe proposed an audacious plan: change the name to Pacific College, sever the relationship with the seminary, and establish a senior college program. The board accepted Wiebe's plan and then hired him as president to carry it out. Pacific College unveiled its new curriculum in the fall of 1960.

The new program had an almost immediate positive effect. Enrollment, which had been declining for over a decade, jumped sharply upward. It increased from 58 to 103 in the first year, reached 257 by 1966, and climbed to 430 by 1971.

Wiebe also set the "new" college on a rapid trajectory toward accreditation. Pacific College received junior college accreditation in 1961 and almost immediately turned its sights toward senior college accreditation. It achieved that goal in 1965, less than five years after having inaugurated its four-year program.

The college hired an almost entirely new faculty during the 1960s, many of them young Mennonite Brethren academics who had only recently received their graduate degrees. This idealistic group of faculty members set out to redefine the theological and cultural orientation of the college. Perhaps the most powerful symbol of that goal was the creation of the "Pacific College Idea" in 1966. This statement, revised in 1982 and 1995, still defines the university's ethos in a profound way.

Though enrollment leveled off in the 1970s, the college introduced new programs during this era that vastly increased its influence and reputation. Most important in this regard were the creation of a teacher education program in 1966, an in-service education program (today known as the School for Professional Development) in 1970, and development of a graduate program in education in 1975. By the mid-1970s, Pacific College had been transformed in ways that made it almost unrecognizable from the perspective of the 1950s.

No single person was more significant in the creation and development of Pacific College than Pres. Arthur J. Wiebe. A former high school principal, Wiebe was pursuing a PhD in mathematics at Stanford University when the Board of Education hired him as a consultant to consider options for the future of Pacific Bible Institute. Wiebe saw little future in the existing Bible institute program and encouraged the board to move aggressively toward a senior liberal arts college program. They not only accepted his proposal, but asked Wiebe to implement his vision as the new president. In that role, Wiebe hired an almost entirely new faculty, oversaw the construction of seven buildings, helped the college achieve accreditation in only about five years, and played an important role in developing its first graduate programs in education. He resigned as president in 1975 but continued to play an important role with the Pacific College Math Project, which later became the Activities Integrating Math & Science (AIMS) Education Foundation.

AUGUST 22, 1960

In the summer of 1960, construction began on dormitories for both men and women (the one-story sections of the present-day Strasbourg and Witmarsum Quads). This would mark the first time that men's dormitory rooms would be on a main campus rather than some remote location. The new dormitories were completed by December, and following the Christmas break, students moved into the new facilities. With these three small buildings on the new campus, Pacific College shut down all operations at Tuolumne Street except for continued use of the pool for physical education classes. Pictured above is construction of the women's dormitory with the seminary building in the background, and below is a finished men's dorm room. On the wall is a Pacific College Vikings pennant, a symbol of the new mascot chosen by students in 1960.

This aerial photograph looking to the east across Chestnut Avenue shows the campus in 1961. The classroom building and small parking lot face Chestnut, with women's dorms behind to the left and men's dorms behind to the right. Farther east is the rough outline of a track and soccer field. Many of the Campus Homesites lots have been built out, though empty

lots still remain along Butler, Townsend, and Heaton Avenues. Much of the surrounding area is still in agricultural production, though two of the college's most significant neighbors are already in place: Twilight Haven to the east and Senior Citizen's Village to the south.

With the closing of the Tuolumne Street campus in January 1961, the three buildings at Chestnut Avenue were required to perform all college functions—a very tall order for such small structures. The library was moved into the classroom building. Cafeteria and dining hall facilities, meanwhile, were set up in the men's dormitory lounge (today, the art studio in Witmarsum Quad). In such a tiny space, meals were very crowded affairs. Meals at this time were served family-style, with serving bowls on the tables rather than a cafeteria serving line. The library remained in the classroom building until 1962, while the cafeteria would not move out of the dorm lounge space until 1964.

While skits and small plays were performed during the PBI years, Pacific College did not produce its first significant theatrical production until 1961. The musical play *Rejected* was performed at the Armenian Hall in downtown Fresno, the Immanuel Academy chapel in Reedley, and Greeley Elementary School near Bakersfield, since the college had no space on campus in which to stage such a performance.

Pacific College's first sign was a simple cinderblock and brick design completed around 1962 facing Chestnut Avenue in the area where McDonald Hall is now located. From left to right, Paula Payne, Jim Becker, and Connie Wiebe visit next to the sign. With only minor modification to the lettering, the sign would stand in this location until about 1989.

These two photographs, both taken in 1963 or 1964, show the new Chestnut Avenue campus during its first few years. The daytime photograph looks along the classroom building walkway toward the men's dormitory, with the buildings of neighboring Twilight Haven visible in the distance. Only one phase of the two-story dormitory section had been completed by this time. The night image shows the men's dormitory in the foreground, women's dorm in the background, and the still-unfinished Alumni Hall barely visible between them. The campus during these years contained large amounts of open space with only minimal landscaping.

Pacific College began intercollegiate athletics programs in 1960, with the creation of a men's basketball program. The first team compiled a record of 5-4 in its first year. Pictured above are coach Gary Nachtigall and the starting lineup of the 1963–1964 basketball team. From left to right are Bob Buxman, Tim Fast, Lloyd Gardner, Richard Frueh, and Don Knaak. In 1962, Pacific added men's soccer. Below, members of that first team lace up their cleats in the men's dormitory courtyard, with phase two of dormitory construction visible in the background. The players from left to right are Dale Jost, Roland Dyck, Willard Martens, Jim Travis, and Helmut Harnisch.

In 1962, the Pacific College commencement took place on the lawn just to the south of the still uncompleted library building. Here, the choir performs under the direction of Dietrich Friesen, with the entire faculty seated on the stage. The class of 1962 graduated 28 students, at least 12 of whom are performing with the choir.

The original dormitories both included a student lounge space. That area was used as a cafeteria from 1961 to 1964 in the men's dormitory, but the women's lounge functioned for its original purpose during that time. Here, three students relax in their lounge, complete with a grand piano.

Hiebert Library was completed in 1962. It was named for Cornelius Hiebert, an office furniture manufacturer who donated most of the money for construction and who also built many of the original furnishings. The original building (shown above) was based on the same design as Tabor College's library, completed in 1957. Below, students study in the main reading area in the 1960s. The card catalog on the left was removed in 1994 when the library implemented an electronic catalog. The library served both the college and seminary, the only department in which those two institutions directly cooperated before the seminary formally joined the university in 2010.

The dormitory buildings (known today as Strasbourg Quad and Witmarsum Quad) were constructed in multiple phases during the 1960s and early 1970s. The one-story sections had been completed already in 1961. In January, the two-story sections on the north side of Strasbourg and south side of Witmarsum were finished. The opposite two-story sections were completed in September 1964, creating two U-shaped buildings. These photographs show the recently completed second phase of Strasbourg (above) and construction of Strasbourg's third phase (below). At this time, Strasbourg was the women's dormitory, and Witmarsum was the men's dorm. Access to the courtyards by the opposite sex (to say nothing of the rooms themselves) was strictly regulated at the time.

The completion of Alumni Hall in May 1964 gave the college its first dedicated cafeteria space on the new campus. The building had a striking Midcentury Modern design, with broad overhanging eaves on the north and west facades and large globe light fixtures on the west. The kitchen and serving line were on the east side of the building, and there were a few small individual rooms on the south side. The remainder of the building was devoted to a dining hall and student lounge. In the early years (as seen here), only about half the room was needed for the cafeteria. As the student body grew, the lounge was removed to make room for a larger cafeteria. Much of the Midcentury Modern aesthetic was lost when the covered sidewalks were enclosed with glass and metal several decades later.

On May 10, 1965, Pacific College received notification that it had been accredited as a senior liberal arts college. When that news reached campus, students and faculty rushed to the airport to meet the president and dean, who were returning from the accreditation meetings in Los Angeles. Students held an impromptu "demonstration" in front of the terminal, marching up and down the sidewalk while holding signs aloft to celebrate the event. The president, dean, and two members of the board rode from the airport back to the campus in a 1965 Chevrolet Impala convertible provided for the event by a local auto dealer. The lead car was followed by a parade of cars driven by students and faculty members. Back on campus, President Wiebe addressed the students from the top of the convertible.

One of the small rooms on the south side of Alumni Hall provided space for the student store, which sold textbooks, supplies, and Pacific College clothing. The student store was moved around campus several times before coming back full circle to occupy the larger space in Alumni Hall where it is located today.

In the spring of 1965, volunteer workers completed an outdoor amphitheater immediately to the west of the men's dormitory. This space became a major gathering place for students. It was the venue for a wide variety of events, including commencement (1965–1982), theatrical productions, concerts, and student life recreational events. It was torn down in 2001 to make room for AIMS Hall.

Lacking an indoor theater or auditorium, the amphitheater served a crucial public events function for several decades, especially in the fall and spring when the weather was conducive to gathering outside. Many drama productions took place here, especially large musicals that once were a common part of the drama department's repertoire. One of the earliest such productions was *Brigadoon*, performed in 1966 (above). Commencement ceremonies also took place in the amphitheater from 1965 through 1982. Below, Vernon Grounds addresses the graduates in 1968, while the faculty are seated on the stage. In the background, the classroom building, women's dormitory, and Alumni Hall can be seen. The Italian cypress trees that would later form the backdrop of the stage had not yet been planted, so potted plants and trees were brought in to provide at least some definition to the stage area.

During the 1960s, freshmen were subjected to a weeklong initiation process. The new students were required to bow to seniors, wear wastebaskets on their heads, carry pillows to class, and generally suffer humiliation in various events led by the sophomores. At right, Bruce Stryd and an unidentified fellow freshman are standing by the campus sign in 1966 wearing beanies and name placards while carrying trash cans. Below, freshmen students in 1965 are being taught a song by the sophomores in the new amphitheater. By the 1970s, it appears that these kinds of initiation events no longer took place.

In May 1965, Pacific College received the entire library collection of Upland College when it ceased operations. The books were transported by truck from Upland to Fresno in June, adding over 23,000 volumes to Hiebert Library and more than doubling its previous size. Here, student Galen Harms (left) and Arthur Wiebe inspect a few of the many volumes piled on the library floor awaiting addition to the collection.

Tucked into the coastal redwood trees between the college and seminary campuses, the Warkentin Prayer Chapel was completed in May 1966. It was dedicated to the memory of Herman Warkentin, who died in India while serving as a Mennonite Brethren missionary. The chapel is never scheduled for classes or other regular events and remains a quiet space for prayer and contemplation today.

Of the many campus buildings completed during the 1960s, none is more original in design than the Science Building (today known as Marpeck Center). Though it appears to be round, the building is actually an icositetragon, or 24-sided geometric shape. While never used exclusively as a science building, it did include specialized classrooms and labs for that purpose, such as the biology classroom below in which Daniel Isaak is teaching. Science classroom and lab space were eventually moved to AIMS Hall when it was completed in 2002. Interestingly, six of the ten vehicles parked in the lot outside of the building above appear to be Volkswagen Beetles.

Pacific College elected its first homecoming court in 1966, another tradition that had not existed during the Bible institute years. Members of the first court were, from left to right, Carol Wiebe, Sharon Toews, Queen Sandy Goertzen, and Elaine Thiessen. The tradition of homecoming courts was rather short-lived and does not appear to have continued beyond the early 1970s.

The Pep Club of 1968–1969 poses for a group photograph in the amphitheater. The Italian cypress trees that would eventually form the backdrop for the amphitheater stage were still very small at the time of this photograph. Only a few of these trees remain today, at the northeast corner of AIMS Hall.

This aerial photograph shows the college and seminary campuses around 1967. College buildings (clockwise from lower left) are the Science Building (later Marpeck Center), the classroom building (later Sattler Hall), Hiebert Library, phases 1–3 of the women's dormitory (later Strasbourg Quad), the maintenance building, phases 1–3 of the men's dormitory (later Witmarsum Quad), Alumni Hall, and the amphitheater. The dirt track and soccer field are on the far right. The seminary campus includes only the original Giffen Home and student apartments to the north of it. Most of the landscaping on the college campus was still quite small, in contrast to the large trees on the seminary campus, most of which had been planted in the 1910s. Hidden by those trees is the Warkentin Prayer Chapel. In the upper right is the Butler Avenue Mennonite Brethren Church sanctuary, which had been completed in 1964 alongside the original fellowship hall.

In addition to many new buildings, two fountains were added to the campus during the 1967–1968 academic year. One was the "Rebekah" fountain, located immediately to the north of the Science Building. Funding for this fountain was donated by music professor Dietrich Friesen and his wife, Anne. This fountain has changed forms over the years. The original statue was removed at some later date, leaving only a water-filled bowl. The family of Dietrich and Anne Friesen later donated funds for a new statue and landscaping around the fountain. The other fountain was built in a plaza area to the west of Alumni Hall. It originally featured a single nozzle as seen below, but was later changed to multiple crosses, then a planter without a fountain, and more recently, a fountain again.

The fourth phase of the men's dormitory (today Witmarsum Quad) was completed in 1968. The photographs here show it under construction and shortly after completion. It was a two-story structure with dorm rooms on the west side and apartments on the east, in addition to a basement. This was the first building on the college campus to have a basement. As was the case in the earlier phases of the men's and women's dormitories, the rooms were arranged into small "modules" rather than simply lining up many dorm rooms on either side of long hallways. In later years, many of the original dorm rooms were turned into offices, first for faculty and later for various administrative departments.

The Witmarsum Quad basement at some point came to be known as "the Pit" and has served a wide variety of purposes over the years. The campus bookstore was moved here fairly soon after construction was completed. At left, bookstore employee Walter Wall is standing at the cash register. The basement also held a large student recreation area, including the billiard tables shown below. Other functions over the years included a television room, laundry facilities, and later, a small theater lab. Today, a large part of the Witmarsum basement is used by the Information Technology Services department as well as video production facilities.

For roughly its first decade, all seminary functions (except the library) were housed in the Giffen Home. That changed beginning in 1966, when the first phase of the Mission Memorial Court (above) was completed to provide seminary student housing. The building, which was completed entirely in 1969, features a plaque in the courtyard with names of Mennonite Brethren missionaries in whose honor it was named. In 1970, the seminary completed construction on the Conference Building (below), which included a chapel, classrooms, and office space for Mennonite Brethren conference agencies (the purpose from which it took its original name). The conference agencies eventually moved out of the building, and it reverted to exclusively seminary use.

Student life at the Bible institute, college, and university has been enhanced by its close proximity to three national parks, none more than a few hours away from campus. Trips to these parks were a regular part of the student experience, such as this group enjoying a picnic in Yosemite National Park during the 1968–1969 school year.

For most of its history, Pacific hired its own food services staff, and the employees tended toward the "Mennonite grandmother" demographic. From left to right, Anne Furioso, Katharine Dick, Alvina Huebert, and Goldie Janzen are at work in the Alumni Hall kitchen, probably in the late 1960s. Today, the university contracts with an external provider for its food services.

During the 1960s and 1970s, athletics opportunities were mostly limited to men. The only team on which women competed was tennis. Records of this program are scarce, but it apparently existed from about 1968 until at least 1971. The 1971 team included (from left to right) coach Jim Powers, Jay Grauman, Sandy Powers, John Warkentin, Milton Miller, Shena Wileman, Larry Waide, Lester Riffel, Barbara Hofer, Bobby Phillips, and Geri Nickel.

The men's cross country program was established in 1966, with six runners. When Woodward Park was founded near the San Joaquin River around 1970, it became a regular site for Pacific's "home" meets. Here, the Pacific College cross country team competes for the first time in Woodward Park against the University of Nevada, Reno, in 1970.

Student programs to support Pacific's athletic programs and generally enhance school spirit have taken a variety of forms over the years. While cheerleaders have not been a continuous presence on campus, they have come and gone over the years. Above, in 1970–1971, the cheerleaders, song leaders, and Viking mascots pose at Fresno's Fulton Mall. From left to right are Mary Hendrickson, Cheryl Unruh, Jim Barnes, Robin Flowers, Jim Miller, Annette Wilson, Kathy McGlory, and Marsha Unruh. Pep bands have also come and gone. At left, a small group of musicians provides support at a soccer game in 1970.

A men's track and field program was organized in 1962 with four team members. This was arguably Pacific College's most consistently successful athletic program during the late 1960s and early 1970s. This photograph from 1971 shows the team during one of its strongest years. The track team produced Pacific's first three National Association of Intercollegiate Athletics (NAIA) individual national champions: Dennis Anderson (shot put, 1972; shown here seated second from right), Steve Hardison (pole vault, 1973 and 1974), and John Turton (discus, 1979). In 1973, the Pacific College track team defeated Fresno State in a two-way meet. The track and field program was eliminated after 1979 and not revived again until 1987. The team pictured here is wearing jerseys that say "Fresno Pacific" even though the college would not adopt that name until 1976. In fact, the sports teams began using the "FPC" label in the mid-1960s, partially at the request of *Fresno Bee* sportswriters who struggled to distinguish it from other schools that used the word "Pacific" in their names.

The women's dormitory became a quad in 1972 with the completion of its fourth phase. While the first three phases of the two dorm buildings were identical, the final phases of Witmarsum and Strasbourg (as they came to be known in 1973) are very different from each other. Strasbourg also had a basement, which over the years has held lounge space, classrooms, student newspaper offices, laundry facilities, and storage.

In 1970, the San Joaquin College of Law began renting classrooms at Pacific College. As the program grew, the law school needed additional dedicated facilities, so it paid for an addition to the east end of Hiebert Library for its law library and faculty offices (shown under construction). The law school moved away in the late 1970s, and this part of the library became the Mennonite Library & Archives.

The fountain plaza to the west of Alumni Hall (first completed in about 1968) received a wooden arbor over it in 1972. This photograph, taken shortly after completion of the arbor and with Alumni Hall in the background, shows the second design for the plaza fountain, which included three crosses rather than a single bowl.

Pacific College offered its first full program leading to a California teaching credential in 1968. The program grew quickly in both size and reputation, and in 1975, the college began offering graduate degrees in education. Many teachers trained at Pacific were hired in Central Valley school districts, including Sandy Wohlgemuth, seen here teaching as part of an intern program at Homan Elementary School in Fresno in the early 1970s.

Like many buildings on the Pacific College campus, Alumni Hall was a multi-purpose space. It was the venue for biweekly College Hour events, such as the one above at which Pres. Arthur Wiebe is speaking in the early 1970s, as well as the concert below during the same era. Since this was the same space used as the cafeteria for three meals a day, the moving of tables and chairs in Alumni Hall was an almost constant occurrence. The drama program also used Alumni Hall for theatrical productions. Since the sets could not be taken down every day to make room for meals, tables sometimes were set up on the temporary stage itself to provide adequate cafeteria space.

The faculty during these years was a tight-knit group. Many had known each other since childhood, and most were members of local Mennonite Brethren churches. Various group activities allowed them to forge a strong sense of community. One such event was a faculty retreat at Hartland Camp, where faculty families gathered for planning and recreation before the school year began. Above, biblical studies professor Edmund Janzen leads faculty members and their spouses in a communion service in the fall of 1972. Other group activities were simply an excuse to be silly. One regular feature of campus life in the 1970s was the Faculty Farce, in which faculty members generally made fools of themselves for the amusement of the students. Below, faculty members sing for the students at a Faculty Farce during the 1972–1973 school year.

As had been true since the earliest days of the Pacific Bible Institute, the Concert Choir remained the centerpiece of Pacific College's music program in the 1970s. The choir regularly sang in local churches and for community groups, and even went on tours to various parts of Europe. Though choirs usually performed wearing formal attire, the camera occasionally captured them in more casual clothing and poses. Above, a choir from the early 1970s under the direction of Larry Warkentin performs at the celebration of the nation's Christmas tree at Grant Grove in Kings Canyon National Park. Below, a choir from the mid-1970s pauses for a group photograph during a retreat in the Sierra Nevada foothills. Director Larry Warkentin is kneeling at lower right.

Three

FRESNO PACIFIC COLLEGE
1976–1997

After vigorous growth during the Pacific College era, enrollment of undergraduate students had stagnated at roughly 400 by the early 1970s. Development of continuing education programs (originally known as "in-service programs") and graduate degrees in education did much to offset the lack of growth in undergraduate programs, but the college found itself again asking questions about its long-term viability. Of particular concern to its denominational supporters, the number of Mennonite Brethren students had started to drop by the late 1960s. While the vision and scope of Pacific College had expanded greatly since the Pacific Bible Institute years, many college supporters still assumed that its primary purpose was to educate Mennonite Brethren young people. If those students were choosing to attend other colleges, what was Pacific College's reason to exist?

Following Arthur Wiebe's resignation in 1975, the new president charged with answering such questions was Edmund Janzen. His answer came in a 1983 document entitled "Broadening the Base," in which he articulated an institutional mission that explicitly extended beyond the Mennonite Brethren Church. He emphasized that the Fresno Pacific College educational experience "simply must be shared with more students—both within the Mennonite Brethren Church and without." Janzen called on the college to vigorously promote its identity, vision, and purpose to a larger constituency. He sought to broaden the college's funding base, create more appointed positions on the board of directors to forge stronger links outside the Mennonite Brethren conference, more aggressively market the college, and recruit more students beyond the Mennonite Brethren Church. The results of "Broadening the Base" were seen first in student enrollment, which began to rise significantly starting in the late 1980s. In 1993, the total number of undergraduate students exceeded 600 for the first time, while total enrollment passed 1,000 for the first time in 1992.

Among the most significant program developments of this era was the creation of the Degree Completion Program. It was centered around a compressed time curriculum for adults that combined course work at the school with credit for life experience, allowing students to complete a bachelor's degree in only 13 months.

The name "Pacific College," used from 1960 until 1976, did little to differentiate the institution from the many other colleges and universities that used the word "Pacific" in their names. Perhaps most confusing in this regard was the University of the Pacific (UOP) in nearby Stockton. The fact that UOP often played Fresno State College in sports during those years only served to heighten local confusion and was part of the reason that *Fresno Bee* sports reporters encouraged the Pacific College athletics program to use the more specific moniker of "Fresno Pacific College." Pres. Arthur Wiebe apparently did not support this new name and thought it was overly provincial. Soon after Wiebe's resignation, however, the college decided to change its name to Fresno Pacific College. The change was made with little fanfare and seems to have gone almost unannounced in any significant way. The sign near the Chestnut Avenue entrance to the campus received new letters, somewhat smaller than the old ones, in order to make room for three words rather than two.

Following Arthur Wiebe's resignation, the college was led for one year by an interim presidential council. In July 1976, biblical studies professor Edmund Janzen (seen here speaking in the amphitheater) was appointed president. Though a member of the faculty, Janzen was also an ordained Mennonite Brethren minister and conference leader, and his appointment represented a return to an earlier model for choosing the college's presidents.

The Chestnut campus remained limited to its original 20 acres until 1977, when the college purchased 18.5 acres to the southeast of Winery and Hamilton Avenues. The new property, named in honor of board member Marvin Steinert of Bakersfield, California, was intended primarily for athletics facilities, though the original plan also included residential lots along Willow Avenue and apartments for married students—neither of which were ever built.

By the 1970s, the music department had added a jazz band to its program. Here, music professor Curtis Funk conducts the jazz band at an outdoor performance during the Fall Festival in 1978. This was the name for homecoming events during the late 1970s and early 1980s. The festivals usually included performances, food, reunions, and a soccer game.

In this photograph from the mid-1970s, students play a game involving an extremely large inflatable ball. The area on which they are playing, known today as the Campus Green, was relatively undeveloped at that time. The old facilities management building is visible in the background. It eventually would be torn down to make room for the Steinert Campus Center.

Since 1954, the Bible institute and college had been governed by a unified board of education that reported to the US Conference of Mennonite Brethren Churches. This board was responsible for the programs of Fresno Pacific College, the Mennonite Brethren Biblical Seminary (until 1975), and Tabor College in Hillsboro, Kansas. Questions about the viability of this unified educational program led to a decision in 1979 to "regionalize" Fresno Pacific College and Tabor and return them to the control of their respective district conferences. In that context, the school once again became affiliated with the Pacific District Conference of Mennonite Brethren Churches, as had been the case from 1944 to 1954. Here, the delegates at the 1979 session of the Pacific District Conference in Bakersfield pose in Fresno Pacific College t-shirts to symbolize their reacceptance of the college as their own. The seminary had already been adopted by the entire North American Mennonite Brethren Church in 1975, and so was not part of this regionalization.

Since 1962, Hiebert Library had been jointly owned and operated by Fresno Pacific College and Mennonite Brethren Biblical Seminary. In 1979–1980, the seminary took responsibility to raise funds for the expansion of the library. The larger building included a two-story section with mezzanine (above), an enlarged main lobby, new archives, and remodeled office area. The new sections were completed before renovation of the existing areas, which allowed the library to remain open during the entire project. Librarians Adonijah Pauls and Steven Brandt were nonetheless forced into rather uncomfortable temporary offices spaces (below) while waiting for new offices to be renovated.

College Hour remained an important part of campus life during the Fresno Pacific College years. College Hours encompassed a variety of programming, including worship events, guest lecturers, student presentations, and performing arts events. These photographs show students gathered in a circle for a worship event during the early 1980s, and a concert by the Bluestein Family from roughly the same time. The Bluesteins—from left to right, Frayda, Jemmy, Evo, and Gene—were a local traditional music group who regularly performed at the college during these years. Since College Hour still took place in Alumni Hall at this time, the ritual of taking down and setting up tables and chairs several times a week remained familiar to everyone.

After disappearing from campus culture in the early 1970s, cheerleaders reappeared briefly a decade later. The cheerleaders for 1980–1981 were (clockwise from left) Meri Aeschbacher, Cheryl Hopkins, Cynthia Siemens, Jill Sorensen, Vicki Stoutingburg, and Karyl Molt. Basketball team members warm up behind the cheerleaders in an unidentified local gymnasium. This would be the last season in which the team was forced to play its "home" games at off-campus venues.

During the 1970s, Mike Vogt was in charge of the facilities management department. Among his legacies were several self-designed implements that were used in the department for many years. Here, facilities employee Kelly Friesen is driving a mobile trash compactor designed and fabricated by Vogt. In later years, these ingenious but unorthodox pieces of machinery were replaced by more conventional ones.

The completion of the Special Events Center (seen here under construction and shortly after completion) in 1981 filled a long-standing gap in the campus infrastructure. Not only did it finally provide a home court for men's basketball and other indoor athletic programs, it also provided a large venue for other kinds of special events.

Completion of the Special Events Center helped make possible the development of women's athletics programs in the early 1980s. Before this time, sports opportunities for women had consisted of only a short-lived tennis program and an occasional individual who competed in track and field or cross country. The volleyball team joined formal intercollegiate competition in 1981, and before the end of the decade, was an NAIA national powerhouse. In the image above, Harriet Huggins is providing inspirational words to her volleyball teammates on the sidelines during the 1983 season. Women's basketball began in 1982. At left, Denise Ainley shoots the ball against Porterville College during the inaugural season while Melinda Clark looks on.

In the spring of 1981, Fresno Pacific College abandoned the Viking as its mascot, replacing it with the Sunbird. The Viking mascot had been chosen through a student contest in 1960. While it was loved by many, others pointed out that neither the college nor Fresno had any historical or cultural connection to Vikings or other aspects of Scandinavian culture. Some critics expressed concern that a mascot generally associated with excessive violence was hardly appropriate for a Mennonite college. After years of such conversations, a committee of faculty, staff, and students was assembled in 1981 to propose a new mascot. The Sunbird was a hybrid (and supposedly imaginary) concept that brought together the two most common suggestions for a new mascot: Fresno's hot summer sun and some kind of bird. Only later was it learned that there actually were such things as sunbirds in Africa and Asia. This photograph of an early Sunbird mascot (which looks nothing like a real sunbird) is wearing a Viking helmet—perhaps evidence that affection for the old mascot had not completely died.

The faculty was still a very small group in the early 1980s, and everyone personally knew each other. Almost the entire group (along with administrators and some staff members) could gather for events such as the weekly Faculty Prayers in a fairly small room during this era. These two photographs capture the entire group in attendance at one such Faculty Prayers session during 1981–1982, meeting in the Strasbourg Quad basement. While not every faculty and administrative member of that time is present in these photographs, most of them are sitting in this one circle.

Among the numerous special events on campus made possible by completion of the Special Events Center, few have been more celebrated than the annual West Coast Mennonite Relief Sale. This event, established in 1966, was held at a fruit packing facility near Dinuba until 1981, when it came to Fresno Pacific College. The gymnasium was turned into a quilt auction venue, while the campus green featured food booths and other items for sale. All proceeds from these sales go to the international relief work of the Mennonite Central Committee. This event remains one of the largest annual gatherings on campus and functions as an unofficial homecoming for many alumni.

Shortly after completion of the Special Events Center, the university installed three flagpoles outside the west entrance. One pole always flies the US flag, another flies the flag of the home country of a current student, and the third, the flag of a country where a former student lives or is working in some kind of service capacity.

From the 1970s until 2005, the Pacific Bookshop was located in the Strasbourg Quad lounge space. At a time when online sales of books had not yet come to dominate the market, the bookshop was known for its extensive inventory, particularly in biblical and religious studies. Here, bookshop manager Richard Wiebe helps a customer find what he needs.

The area between Alumni Hall and Strasbourg Quad was simply an open lawn until the 1970s, when trees were first planted there. By the early 1980s, when this photograph was taken, the trees had become large enough to offer at least some shade for students at picnic tables. Only later would these trees become large enough that students would refer to this area as "the Forest."

Several faculty and administrators began planning in the late 1970s to create a college facility in the Sierra Nevada mountains. They purchased, dismantled, and stored an old cabin located near Kings Canyon National Park. The group later purchased five acres near Shaver Lake, where they rebuilt the cabin, which came to be known as Casa Pacifica. Groups from the college began using it during the 1982–1983 academic year.

The seminary completed a major campus expansion in 1982 (above), with the completion of a classroom wing to the Conference Office Building (today known as North Hall). The wing included three classrooms, a large lounge area with kitchen, and basement recreation area with several other small rooms. The major rooms were named for states and provinces from which the seminary had received significant contributions to fund the construction. The three classrooms were named for California, Manitoba, and Oklahoma. The lounge was named for British Columbia and the basement area for Ontario. Below, seminary students sing in a men's chorus under the direction of Prof. Larry Martens at the dedication event for the new wing.

On pleasant spring afternoons, the allure of the outdoors sometimes became irresistible to both students and their instructors. On those days, the amphitheater often became a temporary classroom. Here, biblical studies professor Devon Wiens (above) and philosophy professor Delbert Wiens (below) teach students in the amphitheater. While the groups pictured here appear to be small upper-division courses, Devon and Delbert Wiens were legendary during the late 1970s and 1980s for the core program courses they taught to first-year students. The original titles of these courses ("World of Priest and King," "World of Prophet and Emperor," and "World of Sage and Messiah") were often abbreviated as "WOPAK," "WOPAE," and "WOSAM," respectively. No one outside of the college had any idea what these acronyms meant.

The amphitheater continued to be the college's major venue for large theatrical productions, such as the 1980 musical production of *My Fair Lady* above. The actors in this scene are, from left to right, Alan Bettis, Sarah Harding, and Terry Clickner. By the early 1980s, however, the amphitheater was no longer large enough to host the annual spring commencement ceremony. The last group to graduate in the amphitheater did so in June 1982, and for the following year, the ceremony moved to the Special Events Center. Below, undergraduate student speaker Stephen Hanselman addresses the graduates, faculty, and guests in 1983.

In 1984, Fresno Pacific College hosted the NAIA national soccer championship tournament. The team was not expected to place highly at the tournament but won every game to advance to the championship match against West Virginia Wesleyan. In a hard-fought game, the Sunbirds lost 3-2 in double overtime, finishing second in the national tournament. In 1985, the Sunbirds again returned to the tournament. They once more advanced to the championship game against the same West Virginia Wesleyan team. This time the match went into four overtimes before the Sunbirds lost by a score of 4-3. In these photographs from the 1984 tournament, Pete Sena goes up for a header against South Carolina, Spartanburg, and goalkeeper Angel Gonzales gets a little rough with a Spartanburg player.

Richard Kriegbaum first became familiar with Fresno Pacific College in 1983 when he served as a consultant to the college. He apparently made a positive impression, since conversations soon began to create a new administrative vice president position designed specifically for him, which he began in fall 1984. When Pres. Edmund Janzen announced his resignation just several weeks later, the presidential search committee almost immediately turned its attention to Kriegbaum, and he was announced as the new president in March 1985. The decision to hire Richard Kriegbaum marked a significant milestone for the school. He was the first president who was not already a member of the Mennonite Brethren Church and had received none of his academic training or ever worked in any Mennonite Brethren institution (other than his few months as a vice president). Kriegbaum served as president until 1997.

The Fine Arts Dinners were significant cultural events on campus from 1986 until the mid-1990s. These events took place in the Special Events Center, featuring a banquet and some kind of musical or dramatic performance. For several years, the event featured music played on the Moore Memorial Pipe Organ, which had been donated to the college by Marguerite Moore in 1980. Renovation and installation of the organ in the Special Events Center were completed in 1986, and the Fine Arts Dinner for that year was its inaugural performance. Above, a crowd is seated around banquet tables at the 1986 dinner. Below, student actors dressed in period costumes pose next to a vintage car at the 1986 event.

In 1986, the college purchased the Haas House, a ranch-style home on a separate lot just to the southwest of the seminary administration building and enclosed with a low brick fence. The house was completely gutted and remodeled for use by the education program. The photograph at left shows seminary student Waldo Berg working on the exposed rafters during the remodeling project. The house originally faced Chestnut Avenue, but this no longer made sense once it became part of the college campus. The orientation of the house was reversed so that its main entrance faced east toward the campus rather than to the west away from it. For its first several years, the building was simply called West Hall, but it later was renamed Bartsch Hall in honor of longtime education professor Silas Bartsch.

The possibility of building a recreational swimming pool was a major agenda item for student government leaders during much of the early to mid-1980s, and finally became a reality in 1987. Above, former president Edmund Janzen and current president Richard Kriegbaum participate in the ground-breaking ceremony during the spring of 1987. In October 1987, the college celebrated the opening of the pool with an event seen in the photograph below. The students who funded the pool always intended it to be for recreational rather than competitive purposes. For that reason, they designed it slightly too short to meet competition specifications. When aquatics programs were introduced a few decades later, however, those teams still took over the pool for practice purposes, thwarting the intention of the students who originally paid for it.

Before 1989, Fresno Pacific sports had produced a few individual national champions and two soccer teams that had fallen heartbreakingly short of championships in 1984 and 1985. But no Viking or Sunbird team had reached the goal of a national team championship. That changed when the 1989 women's volleyball team won the NAIA national championship in Laie, Hawaii, by defeating Hawaii Pacific University in the final match. In these photographs of action from the tournament, Sevy Berryman (No. 5) hits the ball over the outstretched hands of opponents, while Jessica Bennett (No. 14) and Melanie Mariano (No. 10) block a shot during another tournament match.

The Pacific College Math Project was established in the early 1970s under the leadership of Pres. Arthur Wiebe and Ron Claassen to improve mathematics instruction in elementary schools. It conducted math education workshops and distributed cassette tape instructional programs. The project evolved into the AIMS Education Foundation in the early 1980s, through a National Science Foundation grant written by Arthur Wiebe and Larry Ecklund. AIMS sponsored summer workshops, which were attended by educators from across the country. Ecklund (above) and Wiebe (below) are seen here leading these summer workshops. The AIMS program remained a part of the graduate education program until 1986, when it was granted independent non-profit status by the board of trustees.

The AIMS Education Foundation funded construction of the Wiebe Education Center, which was completed in two phases between 1989 and 1993. The two-story building wrapped around the west and north sides of Bartsch Hall along Chestnut Avenue. It housed the AIMS offices and provided office and classroom space for the college. Below, from left to right, Nadine Bartsch, Silas Bartsch, Richard Kriegbaum, Evelyn Wiebe, and Arthur Wiebe participate in the ribbon-cutting ceremony for the completion of phase one in January 1990. The Wiebe Education Center was the first completely new building erected on campus since the Special Events Center in 1981, which was the longest period without such a project since campus construction had begun in 1958.

The Chestnut Avenue campus had no significant architectural focal point for over 30 years. The Chestnut Avenue entrance featured wide stretches of open space, with buildings spaced widely and mostly back from the street. Several of those buildings resembled elementary school facilities more than a college campus. Administrative and student service offices were scattered across virtually every building on campus, and almost all of them were multi-purpose. That unfortunate reality changed significantly in 1992 with the completion of McDonald Hall. The new building, facing prominently onto Chestnut Avenue, gave the campus a central focus point in a way that had never been the case before this time. It brought together under one roof most administrative offices, many faculty offices, admissions, registrar, business, and financial aid offices. The building was named for Arthur and Barbara McDonald, who played a central role in raising funds for the building's construction.

McDonald Hall was constructed with tilt-up concrete walls (seen here from the west side), the only structure on campus ever built in that manner. The two-story atrium on the south end of the building (below) not only housed admissions, financial aid, and registrar's offices in a single area, but also provided a venue for campus receptions and a new performance space on a campus that still lacked adequate facilities for that purpose. Several faculty and staff offices line the second-story perimeter of the atrium, with windows overlooking the open space below.

In 1990, Fresno Pacific College created the Center for Adult Learning, a program to help adults with some previous college credit complete a bachelor's degree in human resources management in only 13 months. The program name was soon changed to the Center for Degree Completion. The first graduating class, which completed the program in spring 1992, included, from left to right, (standing) Frederica Jones, Shanti Marie, Barbara McDonald, Grace Peters, Barbara Raibley, Lisa Clemens, Beatrice Hensleit, Zora Wilcher, Holly Read, and Edith Thiessen. Seated are program director Dennis Langhofer (left) and Shoua Moua. From this small start, the degree completion program would grow to include several other degree programs, offer classes at multiple regional campuses, and enroll a larger number of students than in the traditional undergraduate and graduate programs.

Fresno Pacific College reached a major milestone in September 1994 when it celebrated its 50th anniversary. A gala celebration event in the Special Events Center during the fall featured a banquet, music by the Tulare Symphony and college jazz band, congratulatory words by college administrators and local dignitaries, a gigantic birthday cake, and lots of balloons.

In 1996, the college built a co-generation plant south of the Special Events Center to provide heating and cooling for the campus. In order to connect buildings to the plant, deep trenches were dug across the entire campus, which made foot traffic very difficult for several weeks. Here, information technology director Dave Bonnar stands in one of the trenches just south of Strasbourg Quad.

Four

FRESNO PACIFIC UNIVERSITY
1997–PRESENT

By the mid-1990s, Fresno Pacific College had undergone a remarkable transformation. Once identified primarily by its traditional undergraduate student body, it had become a much more diversified institution. By 1997, traditional undergraduate enrollment comprised less than half of the total student enrollment for the first time. Graduate programs, begun in the field of education in the mid-1970s, were expanding into other disciplines. In 1994, the college had introduced an Individualized Master of Arts Program, which allowed students to create specialized programs based on their own academic goals. In the following year, graduate programs were introduced in Administrative Leadership and Conflict Management & Peacemaking. Other graduate programs have been added since that time. The professional development programs, meanwhile, had been offering continuing education units to professionals in a variety of fields for almost 30 years. More recently, the university expanded its degree completion programs, which had grown from an initial group of 58 students in 1991 to 159 by 1996. This increasing complexity was a major factor in the decision to change names once again, this time to Fresno Pacific University. The new name was adopted in January 1997.

The years since 1997 have been characterized by enrollment growth, increasing diversity among the student body, and development of new programs. Traditional undergraduate enrollment, which stood at 584 in 1997, exceeded 1,000 in 2005. Graduate enrollments have also increased, though not at the same pace. The most significant increases have been in the degree completion programs, most of which have been offered at the various regional campuses. Degree completion enrollment was 138 in 1997 and exceeded 1,000 in 2010. Total enrollment reached 2,000 in 2009 and soared to more than 3,000 in 2011.

Student diversity has also been a major change during the university era. Total racial and ethnic minority enrollment was 24 percent in 1997, with 16 percent of those students being Hispanic. By 2008, the minority enrollment had reached 40 percent and now exceeds 60 percent. Hispanic students continue to be the largest group within that category, and make up roughly half of the total student body today.

In 1997, Fresno Pacific College became Fresno Pacific University. The new name was an acknowledgment of its more complex academic and institutional structures and a symbol of its growing regional reputation. Unlike the 1976 name change, this one was recognized with a celebratory ceremony in the Special Events Center. Here, student body president Sarah Steckling speaks at the ceremony while Pres. Richard Kriegbaum and board chairman Eugene Enns look on.

The first new president of the university era was Allen Carden, appointed in 1997. He had been president of Spring Arbor College in Michigan and before that was a history professor and administrator at Biola University. Carden's tenure as president was fairly short, and he resigned in 2000. Carden later returned to Fresno Pacific University (FPU) and played a major part in the degree completion liberal studies program.

For almost 30 years, the facilities management (or maintenance) department had been housed in a humble corrugated metal shed just to the east of Witmarsum Quad. That building was torn down in 1997 after the completion of a new facilities management building (above) adjacent to the Steinert Athletic Complex southeast of Hamilton and Winery Avenues. The department jokingly made the old building available to be moved, as shown in the photograph below, but apparently, no one took them up on the offer. The new building included two stories and much more extensive facilities for shops, storage, and offices.

East Hall was completed in October 1998. While most of it was used for student dormitories and apartments, the building also included classrooms and offices for various academic programs. At five stories, it was the tallest building ever constructed on campus. During the 2016–2017 academic year, the building's name was changed to Jost Hall, in honor of Chester and Clella Jost of Bakersfield, California.

Harold Haak was appointed president in 2000. A former president of California State University, Fresno, Haak was a highly respected educational leader in the Central Valley. Though not identified as an interim president, Haak never planned to remain in the position for more than a few years. He returned to retirement in 2003.

The track and field program, which experienced considerable success in the early 1970s, was terminated after the 1979 season. The original dirt track was removed to make space for the Special Events Center, and so there were no facilities on campus for the new program when it was revived in 1987. That problem was resolved in 2001 with the completion of a track on the east end of the Steinert Athletic Complex. Unlike the original track and field program, the new program had full teams for both women and men. Fresno Pacific University hosted the NAIA outdoor national championships in 2006 and 2007.

AIMS Hall, completed in 2002 on the site of the old amphitheater, is the home of the university's mathematics and science programs. The building was funded through a donation from the AIMS Education Foundation and includes classrooms, laboratories, and faculty offices. A prominent feature in the building's main lobby is a Foucault pendulum, one of only about 18 in California. Such pendulums are named after French physicist Léon Foucault, who devised the first one in 1851 to demonstrate the earth's rotation. While the pendulum appears to navigate a complete circle as it knocks down pins arranged around it, the earth is actually revolving around the pendulum.

Athletic opportunities for women expanded significantly during the university years. In 2001, a women's soccer program was established, and the team gathered for this informal group portrait during their inaugural season. The soccer facilities for both women and men were moved inside the track in 2001. Lighting was installed in 2006, which made night soccer matches possible for the first time.

Undergraduate Research Days, typically held in the AIMS Hall atrium during the spring semester, are an opportunity for students to exhibit the results of research conducted during that academic year. This photograph, taken from the second floor of AIMS Hall in 2007, shows the display panels arranged around the atrium while students, faculty, and other guests discuss the projects.

D. Merrill Ewert was appointed president of Fresno Pacific University in 2003. He was the first university president since Edmund Janzen to have been raised in the Mennonite Brethren Church and was a graduate of Tabor College in Kansas. Prior to his appointment as president, Ewert had served as an administrator at Cornell University. He was instrumental in creating new administrative structures that helped the school move into the university era. Below, Ewert greets new students and their families on the Campus Green at Acceptance Night in March 2010. This was an event to celebrate new students who had recently been accepted to enroll in classes in the fall.

The Steinert Campus Center (above), completed in 2003, provided new food services facilities, meeting rooms, offices for the Student Life department, and student recreation and lounge areas. It is named for the family of Marvin and Nadene Steinert of Bakersfield, the same family for whom the Steinert Athletic Complex is named. On the south side of the building is a small amphitheater (below). Much smaller and less centrally located than the original amphitheater, the new amphitheater has not played the same role in campus life as its predecessor.

The completion of the Steinert Campus Center in 2003 allowed the university to move its food services operations out of Alumni Hall. No longer needed for its original purpose, Alumni Hall became the new home of a coffee shop and lounge, the campus bookstore (formerly located in Strasbourg Quad), and the mail center (formerly located in Sattler Hall). While completely renovated, the brick walls, fireplace, and ceiling beams still evoke memories of the original building design from 1964. In its new form, Alumni Hall functions as one of the favorite public meeting spots on campus.

The Harold and Betty Haak Tennis Complex, completed in 2005, was a major addition to the university's athletic facilities. Before this time, the only tennis facilities had been a pair of courts located east of Strasbourg Quad that were torn down to make room for Jost Hall. Completion of this complex made possible the establishment of men's and women's tennis teams, which experienced considerable success in the following years.

While most teaching and learning occurs in traditional classroom settings, students often have opportunities to enhance their educational experience in other settings. Here, members of the art club visit the J. Paul Getty Museum in Los Angeles in 2008 with faculty advisors Chris Janzen (center front) and Rebecca McMillen (upper right).

For many years, the annual Thanksgiving lunch in the Special Events Center has been a highlight of campus life. Members of various offices often sit together at the lunch and sometimes decorate their own tables based on a theme for that year. A unique feature of the lunch is the Parade of Nations, in which a student representative from each country represented in that year's student body marches into the Special Events Center carrying the flag of their country. The flags are then displayed across the balcony area, a symbol of the diverse nationalities represented in Fresno Pacific University's student body.

It has long been a tradition for faculty members to line up after commencement ceremonies in two rows and applaud the graduates as they walk out between those rows. It is a time for congratulatory handshakes, high fives, hugs, smiles, and even tears as faculty and students reflect on their time together during the previous few years.

Biblical studies professor Brian Schultz (with back to camera) uses active learning techniques in a 2010 course to teach living biblical Hebrew. This innovative approach to learning the biblical Hebrew language teaches students to learn Hebrew in the same way that they learned their first language as a small child.

The degree completion program, established in 1990, quickly attracted attention in other Central Valley communities, and the university began to receive requests to offer courses in some of those places. Cohorts of students were set up in Visalia (1992), Bakersfield (1996), and Merced (1996). At first, those cohorts met in short-term rented locations, but eventually, the university found it necessary to set up more permanent facilities. In January 2005, the Visalia Regional Center (above) opened on Cypress Avenue, and the Bakersfield Regional Center (below) opened on Truxton Avenue. While called regional centers at first, the names were later changed to regional campuses.

While a regional campus in Fresno might have seemed superfluous for a university already located in that city, Fresno Pacific University nonetheless established a North Fresno Campus in the River Park area of the city in December 2005. The rapidly growing degree completion programs had outstripped the capacity of the main campus, and the university found it beneficial to have a presence in the northern part of the city in addition to its main campus in southeast Fresno. Located in leased space in one of the most important commercial districts of Fresno, the North Fresno campus featured amenities unfamiliar to the main campus, as seen below in its main lobby.

The women's volleyball team remained a national powerhouse for many years after its initial championship in 1989. Its period of greatest NAIA dominance came during the years 2007–2010, when it won the national championship for four consecutive years. Above, team members accept the trophy and plaques for their victory in the 2007 tournament in Columbia, Missouri. Below, they display the championship banner following their victory in the 2008 tournament in Sioux City, Iowa. The 2009 team finished the season with a perfect 38-0 record and won the 2010 title without dropping a single set in the entire national tournament.

The land for new athletics facilities stood empty for the first few years after its purchase in 1977. Construction there first took place in 1980 when a new soccer field was completed on the far west end to replace the one that had been on the site of the Special Events Center. The rest of the land remained undeveloped, except for an old farmhouse on Willow Avenue. In subsequent years, the Steinert Athletic Complex grew immensely, both to better serve existing athletics programs and in response to the development of new programs. This aerial photograph of the complex shows its current configuration. In the foreground on the right are the Facilities Management Building and parking lot. Next to that is the baseball stadium (completed in 2007). Immediately beyond it is the Harold and Betty Haak Tennis Complex (2005). On the far east end of the complex near Willow Avenue are the track and field facilities (2001), inside of which is the Ramirez soccer field (2001).

Degree completion and graduate programs at the regional centers grew rapidly in the first decade of the 21st century, and the programs in Visalia and Bakersfield both outgrew their first locations. They moved into new, more spacious buildings in 2009. The Visalia Regional Campus (above) relocated to Plaza Drive, while the Bakersfield Regional Campus (below) moved to River Run Boulevard. More recently, the Bakersfield programs have moved to a new location at Bakersfield Christian High School on Stockdale Highway.

The degree completion and graduate programs in Merced moved into their own dedicated regional campus building on El Portal Drive in 2011 (above). The regional campus programs remain a highly successful part of Fresno Pacific University's program and have seen the greatest growth in student enrollment. The small cohorts designed to accommodate the needs of working adults appeal to many students for whom a traditional university structure is simply not feasible. Below, professor Peggy Avakian teaches a class at the North Fresno campus in 2008.

The Business Forum was established in 1999. Originally events in which local business leaders and members of the Fresno Pacific University community discussed economic and development needs in the Central Valley, the forums later featured nationally known speakers from the business world. In 2003, the Business Forum hosted legendary college basketball coach John Wooden, seen here (seated) on stage with Pres. Merrill Ewert.

The first Central Valley Ministry Forum took place at Fresno Pacific University in 2004. These events featured influential national church leaders addressing topics relevant to ministry to the Central Valley and larger world and have drawn a large audience from the Central Valley church community. Here, 2010 Ministry Forum speaker John Ortberg addresses over 500 attendees in the Special Events Center.

Ever since it adopted the Sunbird as its mascot in 1981, the university has struggled with the perennial question, "Just what does a Sunbird look like?" The committee that chose the mascot had no idea that sunbirds were even a real thing, and so assumed that any visual depictions would be based on imagination alone. The discovery that sunbirds actually existed did not help much since they are a small, colorful group of nectar-feeding African and Asian birds—hardly the stuff of majestic athletic symbols. As a result, the athletic department has continued to let imagination dictate how the Sunbird is depicted, as seen in these mascot costumes from 2009 (right) and 2015 (below).

During the university era, the music program expanded to include many more instrumental programs. Here, Roy Klassen conducts the concert choir and band at a performance in 2008 at the Paul Shaghoian Memorial Concert Hall at Clovis North High School. Other instrumental ensembles during this era included a bell choir, baroque orchestra, and string quartet.

Music and drama programs were performed in a wide variety of locations on a campus that lacked a performing arts center. For several years, the Ashley Auditorium on the north end of McDonald Hall was the most common venue for theatrical productions, such as this 2006 performance of *Spirit of Hispania*. Actors shown here are Noé Hernandez (left), Michael Chavez (standing center), Crystal Lopez (seated center), and Stephanie Wasemiller (right).

University commencements had outgrown the original amphitheater by the early 1980s and moved into the more spacious Special Events Center. Even that venue had become too small in just a few years, forcing students to invite only a small number of guests. While overflow guests were able to watch the event on video screens in Steinert Campus Center, such remote participation was far from satisfactory. In 2002, commencement was held on the former soccer field on the west end of the Steinert Athletic Complex. A more suitable outdoor location was the campus green, between Jost Hall and Steinert Campus Center, as seen in this photograph of the 2010 ceremony taken from the roof of Jost Hall. While the outdoor venues provided adequate seating for guests, they also courted the risk of rainy weather (rare in May) or hot sun (common in May).

The Sunbirds added swimming and diving programs in 2007, utilizing the aquatics facilities at nearby Sunnyside High School for their home pool while practicing in the campus swimming pool next to the Special Events Center. Above, the women's 200-medley relay team (from left to right, Lauren Malthaner, Stacy Carter, Cheyenne Coffman, and Christine Dillon) smile for the camera after finishing second at the NAIA national championship in St. Louis on March 5, 2009. Below, the men's swimming and diving teams celebrate winning the 2010 NAIA national championship in St. Peters, Missouri. This was the first national championship won by any Sunbirds aquatics team.

In addition to swimming and diving, the Sunbirds also added water polo teams in 2007 (men's) and 2008 (women's). Like their other aquatics counterparts, the water polo teams used Sunnyside High School as their home pool. Above, Nonie-Ann Grant celebrates with teammates during a women's water polo match. The other significant addition to the athletics program during this era was men's baseball. The team began competitive play in 2006 and began playing on a new campus baseball diamond in the Steinert Athletic Complex in 2007. Below, the 2017 team is captured in its own celebratory moment.

Though they shared the campus and library, the seminary and university had been separate institutions since 1960. That arrangement ended in 2010, when the seminary became a part of Fresno Pacific University. Formerly known as Mennonite Brethren Biblical Seminary (MBBS), it changed its name to Fresno Pacific University Biblical Seminary. This photograph shows the temporary sign that was erected to announce the change.

At an event to celebrate the relationship between the university and seminary in 2010, all living presidents of the two institutions gathered for a group photograph. From left to right are (first row) Merrill Ewert (FPU), Henry H. Dick (MBBS), and Elmer Martens (MBBS); (second row) Lynn Jost (MBBS), John Toews (MBBS), Larry Martens (MBBS), and Arthur Wiebe (FPU); (third row) Edmund Janzen (FPU), Allen Carden (FPU), and Henry Schmidt (MBBS).

Pete Menjares became president of Fresno Pacific University in 2012. Menjares was widely respected as a consultant on intercultural competencies in the university environment. He was the first Latino to serve as FPU's president. He brought a warm, pastoral presence to his role as president, and was well-received by students and local churches and in the larger community. But his tenure as president was brief, and he resigned in 2014.

In its ongoing quest to find the ideal commencement venue, in 2014, the university went to Chukchansi Park in downtown Fresno, the home stadium of the Fresno Grizzlies baseball team. While this venue offered ample seating and a novel setting, the perils of outdoor events were evident at this ceremony in a new way. Brisk winds forced many participants to hold tightly to their graduation caps.

Fresno Pacific University's current president is Joseph Jones, who accepted that position in 2017. During the interim after Pete Menjares's resignation, former president Richard Kriegbaum returned to the presidency for about three years until Jones was appointed. Jones was previously vice-rector at Forman Christian College in Lahore, Pakistan. Before that, he was provost at North Park University in Chicago and a dean at Messiah College in Pennsylvania.

In recent years, Fresno Pacific University has moved its commencement ceremonies to Selland Arena in downtown Fresno, a venue with more than adequate seating and none of the risks that come with an outdoor location. The university holds two commencement events each year, one in early December and another in early May.

As Fresno Pacific University celebrates 75 years, generations of graduates, students, faculty, administrators, staff, board members, and supporters can be proud of what they have accomplished, and welcome accomplishments to come. Their history is a legacy of possibilities that invigorates their faith and resolve. They look to the future, confident graduates will explore new pathways with courage, knowledge, and hope. Christ was the foundation when the doors of Pacific Bible Institute opened September 18, 1944, to 28 students and has remained so through the changes as it became first a junior college, then a four-year college, and today a university and seminary awarding bachelor's, master's, and certificates at five campuses stretching from Merced to Bakersfield as well as online. The vision of Christian higher education is embodied in the university's "Idea"—a charge to this learning community to fill minds with knowledge and hearts with faith, so their graduates embody justice, reconciliation, service, and humility. Through all that has happened and in all that will, they remain confident that with God, all things are possible.

Visit us at
arcadiapublishing.com